BLUE WOLVES

Poems
and
Assemblages
by
Regina O'Melveny

for Pat
walking with
words,

best,
Regina O'Melveny

BLUE WOLVES
Poems
and Assemblages

Regina O'Melveny
1996-97 Winner
Bright Hill Press
Poetry Book Award
Chosen by Michael Waters

Cover Art: "The Oracle of Four O'Clock " by Regina O'Melveny
Cover and book design by Bertha Rogers

Editor in Chief: Bertha Rogers
Associate Editor: Graham Duncan
Editorial Intern: Scot Alan Slaby
First Readers: Graham Duncan, Mike Krischik, Scot Alan Slaby

Blue Wolves is published by Bright Hill Press.

Editorial Address: Bright Hill Press
PO Box 193
Treadwell, NY 13846
Voice: 607-746-7306 / Fax: 607-746-7274
Electronic Mail: wordthur@catskill.net

Printed on acid-free, recycled paper in the United States
by the Courier Printing Company, Deposit, New York

ISBN: 0-9646844-7-0
FIRST EDITION

ACKNOWLEDGMENTS

Some of these poems first appeared in the following publications:

"Blue for Dying, Red for Death," *Bringing Hope to a Hopeless World* Anthology
"Blue Wolves" and "Leaf Mask," *California State Poetry Quarterly*
"The Locust, the Bee, and the Spider," *Dreamworks*
"The Butterfly Collector," *Electrum*
"Meteora," *Iris, A Journal for Women*
"The Green God," *Jacaranda Review*
"Wei Chi," *Poetry/LA*
"Bees, after Chernobyl," *The Sculpture Gardens Review III*
"The Yellow Brush," *South Coast Poetry Journal*
"Vanessa Cardui," *Spreading the Word,*
Winners of the LA Poetry Festival Contest
"Divination," *West/Word*
"The Second Fox," *Wild Duck Review*
"Artichokes," "She Considers Love with a Man Already Pregnant
with Another Woman," and
"She Does the Red Dress Dance," *Yellow Silk.*

------

*My thanks to the Cummington Community of the Arts for their
support of me as a writer and as a mother.*

for Bill, Adrienne, and Ursa, wild friend

CONTENTS

THE SEASON OF MIRRORS

THE SEASON OF BALANCED SIEVES, BALANCED HATCHETS

THE SEASON OF BONES

THE SEASON OF BLUE WOLVES

ASSEMBLAGES BY REGINA O'MELVENY

THE SEASON OF MIRRORS

THE HAND-HELD MIRROR

I
Sir Francis Drake Highway

Late at night a deer
streaks through the swath
of my headlights
as I swerve and miss,
glimpse her
in the rearview mirror,
catch the rustling
of Queen Anne's lace and hemlock,
as the deep blue shutters
of night close behind me.

The deer sweeps through me
like the gleam
of a hand-held mirror
from a second-story window years ago
when an unseen woman
turned to observe
the back of her hair
and arced light across my path.
I stood in the dark cobbled street
beneath the wrought-iron window,
the secret source of light.

II
Nicasio Valley Road

Midnight and the neon white eyes
of a doe from a long way off.
She holds her ground
full in the center of the road,
yellow slashes running on beneath her.
I slow to a stop, extinguish my lights.

The woman with the hand-held mirror
comes to meet me, her soft brocade dress
moving in abundant folds around her.
I think she may give me the looking glass.
Instead she turns, invites me to follow.
In the umber thickness of her hair at the nape,
she has fastened a small oval mirror
like women in the mysteries,
so that each one may see herself in the other.

The doe moves off the road, dips her head
to the waiting darkness of trees
where the others, now visible,
wait to see what I will do,
watch with keen silver eyes.

III
Highway One

I don't see the shadow-gray buck
until I've passed
and he leaps away from the corner of my eye.
I turn the car around,
park in the pungent weeds
and step into the tree-ringed field,
my ankles drenched with damp
from sweet grass and mallow
as dusk deepens into cobalt.
I walk the field many years,
letting fall bits of clothing, earrings, and shoes.
When I reach the stag
and feel the wet heat of his breath,
I am ready at last
to step into the ochre light
that glances
from the keyhole darkness of his eyes.

AURELIA AURITA

I

I ask the aquarium attendant for a chair
so I may sit and watch *Aurelia aurita*,
moon jellyfish in the planktonkreisel,
"world without corners" where currents
are described by her drift.
She is the thinnest veil, amniotic,
nuptial, a hymen revolving in liquid space.
O membrane of possibilities, bell resounding underwater,
eight-lobed blossom of luminous life-gel
dangling four sleeves in the shape of a sauvastika —
"so be it" in Sanskrit, that terrible sign
of our century reversed in her body moonwise,
as she rises in three languid pulses.

II

I am in love with her doubled transparent dome,
inverted quartz bowls, one inside the other.
She rings in the dense dark, holds her form there.
I have also seen her washed up on sand,
a collapsed plastic bag with the moon drained out of her.
I have seen the blank night sky flicker
with stars already extinguished,
a light that sifts down like spent brine shrimp.
All I have to eat is illusion.
The aquarium is closing.

III

Still she stays with me, the flared mandala skirt,
the hem frayed with fine tentacles
that sport a slight sting for prey,
the radial veins like seams stitched out from her pouches,
four white omegas that bloom at the center of her hunger.
I too want my desire to be balanced at the core
extending to the four directions.
I want her sexual phosphorescence,
yellow and violet ripe female. She holds her eggs
gleaming white on long oral arms, as she casts
for jettisoned sperm in the random brine soup
where miraculously, bits of avid life find each other.

6 - *Blue Wolves*

SHE DOES THE RED DRESS DANCE

She does the red dress dance, sudden topaz turn, pallid bellies
of a thousand frogs dance,
the bishop's croziered two-step, nightmare's leap, pale nun's
severed black tresses dance,
the centaur's heel and hoof, telluric crystal pose, Luna moth shudder,
the broken hands dance, caves of Barcelona step, Dicte candle spiral
    down,
the white light wave and particle waltz,
the hand of Fatima feathered unfurl, nausea undulation,
driven Dervish swirl,
the lover's razor cumbia, Delphic dust hasapiko, Piacenza bronze
    routine,
the apples of the black sun dance, Pontian tik, buttock flap,
the slippery island tarantella, slim fish of sadness slide,
the hot bride's bounce and cool gavotte,
the clot in the heavy Aztec heart dance,
swift tongue tango, alchemist's coil, widow's cyrto, catacombed creep,
the gold-coined shake and Minerva-bright roll,
the damp place under one hundred breasts dance,
sand draining time and sweet fortune samba,
the red dress, the red dress dance.

THE HUNGER OF THE CECROPIA

After the hot rain,
big drops splotch the stone steps
in the summer garden.
A caterpillar, sapling-green,
thumbs the sky.
She is covered with fantastic tubercles
tipped with yellow, blue, and red.
The cecropia sways and reveals
her great mouth parts
designed for ravening leafy flesh,
sucking elm, birch, and ash.
Such fabulous appetite.
And after the splendid season of glut,
a dry cocoon and winter fast.

In spring after dogwood opens
white four-winged blooms,
the pupa gnaws her crisp shroud,
wriggles free into night,
dusky fields with pale lunules.
Her vestigial mouth parts useless,
the moth voraciously seeks a mate,
lays her glistening eggs.
Then she hungers only for light,
wings worn to transparency
as she buffets the lambent window
she becomes.

THE NATURAL ADAPTATION OF THE VIPER

When I visit my sister Anna,
she says the local Umbrian viper
that lives in the green heart of Italy
is so venomous
the mother must climb
the blackberry canes and drop
her live young to earth.
Otherwise, nesting, they kill each other.
I think it should be
this way in our family.
My sister says
a person bit by a viper
has one half hour
to receive the antidote or die.
Her friend Tommaso survived the bite,
but constantly twitches
his head to the left.
The thing about the viper, says Anna,
is that it gives no warning
and doesn't move out of your way.
As we walk the dirt path
bordered by stones latticed with vetch,
I glimpse the gray viper spill
from a crack in the wall.
The viper is compelled to strike
because venom builds up in its fangs.
We pass close to our mother's house
but we will not go in.
Tomorrow, my sister says
we can pick blackberries.

THE BUTTERFLY COLLECTOR

The butterfly collector was lost in Mexico.
      My father left when I was nineteen.
They searched for a week before they found him.
      I waited fifteen years.
The body in the jungle was black and swollen.
      I couldn't remember his face anymore.
His pockets bulged with 20,000 pesos.
      I wanted to recover our words.
They couldn't understand why he had so much cash.
      He never wrote a single letter.
The collecting bag was still on his back.
      I accumulated silence.
Inside there was a killing jar, mounting board, and pins.
      My father never wanted us to change.
The specimens were fragile and well-preserved.
      The family fell apart.
The net was abandoned, snagged on a stump.
      Later he tore up whole landscapes, his paintings.
The doctors said he died of thirst and starvation.
      My father grew thin, gray, and bitter.
Yet the trees were laden with fruit.
      He simply disappeared.
The relatives came to identify the body.
      My grandmother says he lives in Canada.
They had to wash the money in the river.
      I want to write a letter to my father.
They couldn't get rid of the smell.
      I can hardly believe he has survived.

LEAF MASK

Over our bed
the wooden mask,
a green leaf god
hisses
from the carved mouth slit,
words like steam
curling from rice fields
after monsoon.

> We whisper
> under enormous leaves
> at the edge of rain forest.
> Trees watch you
> press me
> against a trunk.
> You dig at the bark,
> green wood underneath,
> to the hard pith of years
> that ring the core.
> I hold you
> like a cut
> I cover with fresh bark.
> You move the scar
> a tough seam
> between us.

The leaf mask is silent.
You tell me
our cedar house will last
through a quake
because wood forgives.

12 - *Blue Wolves*

THE ELK HEART LINE

Elk,
this is a song of thanks.
Seven years back, you clambered down
to the road before me
from the steep granite scarp,
knees buckled under from the fall.
You rose and faced me,
dark-chested, tree-antlered,
earth-muscled elk.
        I give thanks
for the way you turned
and crossed the valley,
leapt fence after fence
while astounded cattle and horses
spun in their small corrals,
stirred by your lunge,
their necks and withers
frothed in sweat.
        I give thanks
for the thick sounds
you drew from my throat,
grunts of awe.
The Zuñi knew these spirit grunts
when they painted you
black on bone-white bowls,
an arrow heart line from mouth to core.
        I give thanks
a bowl full of words
for what cannot truly be spoken
yet sings, leaps

THE SEASON OF BALANCED SIEVES, BALANCED HATCHETS

DIVINATION

from *Roget's Thesaurus*

by oracles, the Bible,
the dictionary,
by ghosts, spirits seen in a magic lens,
shadows or manes,
by appearances in the air,
the stars at birth,
meteors, winds,
by sacrificial appearances,
the entrails of fishes,
by sacrificial fire,
red-hot iron,
smoke from the altar,
by mice, birds,
a cock picking up grains,
by fountains, fishes,
herbs, water, a wand,
by the dough of cakes,
meal, salt, dice, arrows,
by a balanced hatchet,
a balanced sieve,
a suspended ring,
dots made at random on paper,
by precious stones,
pebbles drawn from a heap,
mirrors, writings in ashes,
by dreams, the hand,
nails reflecting the sun's rays,
finger rings, numbers,
drawing lots,
by passages in books,
the letters forming
the name of the person,
by the features,
the mode of laughing,
ventriloquism,
by currents,
dropping melted wax into water,
by walking in a circle.

THE YELLOW BRUSH

Fifty feet high
the painter adjusts
the strap that holds him
to the steel girder.
He switches brushes,
strokes on bright canary yellow
as he inches backwards.

When he pauses,
shakes out a cigarette,
the brush comes loose
from his belt,
sails over the side,
migrant bird
that dives downwind,
strikes the earth at my feet.

I tug at a dandelion
in my garden,
my shoes spattered yellow.
This is the first day
of autumn.
All things balanced
have just slid
over the edge.
Leaves tear off
in my hands.
I can't get the roots.
The light is going.
Only the tall
unfinished building
catches the sun,
a sad gold grid
against night.

A PACKET OF EGGS

My body holds eggs,
two spoonfuls of flickering opals
like those I bought in Bangkok
when a slim-fingered woman wrapped them
in cream-colored tissue,
the cabochons I tucked in my pocket
and fingered like translucent milk teeth.

My body moves eggs,
small pebbles that dig in
my pelvic slough
as they work downstream.
I grow older, closer to the mineral world,
hardening of the arteries,
gallstones, kidney stones,
the need to eat iron and calcium.

What was once a small pain
now doubles me over.
Something in me has grown lithic.
Opals at the lips of hot springs
crystallize bone and wood
that would otherwise disappear.
I preserve what is already lost.

Since birth I have carried my measure,
let slip one by one the hidden ova,
like a treasure leaked out
through a hole in the pocket.
The doctor scans my organs with sound.
She cannot diagnose my pain.

Opals are said to clear the mind,
give foresight and ward off the evil eye.
Now as my eggs push through me,
I unfold and release the fire
in the stones that ache to be born.

THE SANDHILL CRANE

The woman dreams a sandhill crane
slips from a mailing tube
onto the floor of the post office,
lies elongated and compressed
from the cylinder.
Its wings relax, fan slightly.
The woman has come for her mail.
Though the tube has no address
she claims the long gray bird,
its thin tapered beak in line
with the elegant body
like a compass needle pointing due North.
Just then a man in a dun uniform,
a letter sorter perhaps,
comes and kneels near the dead crane,
cuts off its wings,
and presents them to her.
Saddened, she tucks the wings under her arm
and leaves the post office.
She has received no letters today.

THE OPOSSUM

I find her at dusk on the road,
a deflated sack of fur,
crushed ribs, vertebrae, skull.
I poke at her with a stick,
stir the dusty debris.
Only a single gnarled paw
and the bald scaly tail are intact.
I pick up the paw that clutches tar,
a diminutive fist in my palm.
Like the opossum, I play dead.
You are not the real danger.
The accident occurs in my body.
I want to learn how to unhinge
my knuckles from asphalt.
I keep the opossum's paw as reminder.
Survival this way could be fatal.

STANDING GRAY

Massachusetts

He says
the best wood for fire
is the standing gray,
dead trees that refuse to fall.
I see them at night
stark in a sag pond,
raspy bones bared
in the dense wood,
the thin bane fingers of crones,
dead Salem women
whose hard patience holds
through trial by water,
fire, and ice.

I am a stranger in August
and know nothing of winter.
My neighbor
already thinks
snow, firewood.
Where I live
a season is mostly a change of light.
The year starts wet, then runs dry
for eight, nine months.

He tells me
the gray burns slow and constant.
Alone in my cabin
I watch him chop wood
behind the white barn.
He leaves a small stack near my door.
Later, September,
I light the first fire,

balance three splits on kindling.
When the fire takes, I hear
brittle voices
released from the heartwood,
and see them outside my window
standing gray
in a field of moon.
How good to know
what burns well.

FALCON

This morning a hawk cries,
marks territory,
and pulls me to my own.
I kneel, a tracker after spoor,
and search the oracular disorder
of leaves, twigs bent in passage,
and dry hawk castings.
I open pellets of rodent fur, skeletons,
insect husks compacted
like the welter of the past.
This perfect field-mouse skull
engages a raspy leg.
The ribs, a brittle hexagram,
enclose a chitinous wing.
I read bits of undigested memory.
My father taught me
how the random coheres
before the practiced eye
and relates a passage or death.
When the hawk cries again

    I hear a falcon.
    My father gives me his leather glove
    dwarfing my awkward hand.
    I am only twelve
    but I push my wrist toward the falcon,
    his notched beak and talons.
    I want to hold the raptor
    who kills with beauty,
    plummets clenched feet forward
    and strikes mid-air,
    drops a pigeon with violent grace.
    The falcon descends

while my father retreats, vanishes.
He knew how to cover his tracks.
The mud impressed
by the grid of a heel,
the thread caught
on the puzzle bark of the pine,
the split edge of a leaf,
are not the signs of my father.
I walk in circles and
carry earth on my soles.
My clothes are knotted with snags.
I lead with the heart
against scrub and tree,
and still I do not find my father.

THE ESPERANZA

The Greek captain of the Libyan ship
was finally abandoned by his crew in Panama.
The vessel Esperanza sat anchored in the port
like an Orinoco toad, the kind whose offspring
gestate on its back, then burst out of its flesh.
My father liked to tell me the story of the toad.
I want to tell him the story of the captain
who sat in his cabin while the engine stalled
just outside the Isthmus with its haul
of Colombian bananas and contraband
concealed in lifeboat cushions, railings, and heads.
Even the diesel tank held submerged goods,
cases of canned Alberta cling peaches, surplus from trade
with Colombian dealers who coveted the fruit.
Then from Port Hueneme, Del Monte sent a telegram:
Dockworkers strike — in negotiation —
will advise soon —stay in Panama — stop.
The captain remained with his ship
though he suspected the sargasso of events
was dispatched by the furies
of his estranged wife and children.
Beneath his polished shoes, the garish green bananas
sweated, yellowed, and blackened by degrees.
When a month had passed, the hold belched a dark liquor.
He could be reduced no further.
The captain packed his bag
and sped toward shore, the virulent swamp.
Some months later the Del Monte agent
wired home from Panama: Found captain —
Las Esclusas Hotel — delivered termination letter — stop.
The captain holed up in the hotel
and wrote long letters that he failed to address
though he dropped them in the mailbox.
They collected in the Dead Letter File
at the tortilleria that doubled as a post office.
I want to tell my father, wherever he is,
the story of the captain.

STOLEN HAIR

Women with long hair in Rio
must cover or twist it into a knot
when they go out in public
or it will be stolen.
Hair thieves stalk the lush heads
of women in sidewalk cafés
as they speak and gesture
with eloquent hands,
read photonovelas, letters from friends,
the poems of Delmira Agostini,
Gabriela Mistral, Alfonsina Storni,
as they savor thick coffee or cognac,
and sample sweet cakes,
their fingers dusted with cinnamon.

The men shadow women
who rest on park benches
shrouded in a green noon,
women who sweat at bus stops
surrounded by thick diesel vapors,
women who stare at the garish posters
announcing Yu Li, a Korean beauty
who hangs by her voluminous hair.

Thieves follow the switches of women
whose clipped steps echo
in tiled courtyards, then stop, scuffle.
Heads are wrenched backwards,
hair razor slashed.
Dealers will peddle their wigs
in Los Angeles, Paris, New York.

When one of the hair thieves
hung himself with a length of hemp,
the women gathered to see
the heaps of trussed hair in his room.
They loosened the strands,
reclaimed long tendrils
for amulets against other thieves.

Now the women move through the city
in fierce mourning, cropped heads bristling
or long braids unbound.
Each woman wears another woman's hair
in her own.

> *Cover your hair or you will draw demons,*
> *cause thunderstorms, and sink ships at sea.*

A REVELATION OF HAIR

I long for Sonia Braga hair,
a dark fountain, live thing,
sea of hair, I Thalassa
the goddess in the painting from Mytilene hair.
Her blue-green mane lifts
the boisterous head of Orpheus,
lulls ships with vining masts,
jostles the chalk-blue skiffs of fishermen
who grope toward canny sirens.

But my hair will not descend
beyond my shoulder blades.
Strands break or curl back on themselves.
Once I copied Indian women
and poured coconut oil on my hair,
which became a greasy rope
and tugged on my scalp for days.
In high school I straightened my hair
with foul-smelling chemicals,
jumbo juice cans, and the iron.

I grew up with illustrations
from the Brothers Grimm,
those princesses with hair
trailing the ground.
At three my locks were glossy springs
my mother wound around her finger.
Her nickname as a child
was *Capellone* or *Big Hair.*
During World War II in Rome
she fled from her brother,
who threatened to shear her head
because she slept with a German.
Her unlucky friends
cornered by Italian men
were shaved to the jeers
of *Pelati!,* the peeled ones.

My mother, brush in hand,
was the keeper of my hair.

I was her little queen,
her ladder, tresses in the tower.
When at thirty-eight, I cut my hair short
and it fell in a great dark mass
on the floor all around me,
I felt my mother fall away,
her brown waves identical to mine,
felt her mother fall away,
her reprimand, "Cover your hair!"

Now my dusky thicket laced with silver
is a serpentine halo I loose in all directions
and let fall where it will.

THE SEASON OF BONES

INTO THE LONGEST NIGHT

Winter solstice

Paul Caponigro's "Running White Deer"
hangs unseen for years on my wall,
until I startle them as I walk at dusk
near Divide Meadow, soaked in coastal fog.
Damp bay laurel sweetens the air.
Fallow deer nudge the darkness
under Douglas fir, Bishop pine,
nuzzle the chill packed earth
for the green light stirring in its heart.
I barely breathe. They fix on me.
We are motionless as the last glow
brings us up like ghosts on a negative.
Then the young leap forward
on spring-loaded legs, dazzling stems of light.
Bucks and does bark the alarm
and all bolt in clipped unison,
luminaries streaming out of range
off the edge of the picture.

WEI CHI / BEFORE COMPLETION

> One must move warily,
> like an old fox walking over ice.
> *The I Ching*

Last year I buried the red fox
under the elm that leaned
from a season of wind.
Struck by a car,
he had stiffened,
grown large with death.

Now I dig up his skeleton,
ask his bones
to speak of the crossing,
ice that covers
the swift black surge,
the river's teeth that clench,
unclench, grind, and creak.

I drop down to paws,
a skittish furred body,
pink-membraned ears.
I move very slowly,
test the cold crust
that hides the iron smell of water.
When a place that felt sure
splits open
something frozen in me
gives way.

I want to know
what the old fox knows
as I sniff out the river,
eye the deep god
in the marrow heart
of my bones,

the twisted current
that threatens to crush me.

I put his bones on my workbench.
At night
the sound of the river
keeps me awake.

MY FATHER'S NUMBER

She slipped me a torn bit of paper
and said, "This is your father's number.
Tell him he'd better get out here.
He won't listen to me."

I stared at my once ample grandmother,
her splotched yellow flesh
a damp curtain stuck to her bones.
She was like the window left at a crazy slant
after the rest of the house has collapsed.

For fifteen years she had known
where my father was, and kept it from me.
I held her arthritic hand, a stiff latch
I wanted to fasten against the wind.

I could have broken her, like rotten wood
but she was already crumbling.
This eighty-two-year-old woman I loved
for her plain and spunky Kansan speech
had slammed her heart shut.

She said, "I did it for him. He asked me
to keep his whereabouts hidden.
He was afraid of your mother.
A woman like a dark funnel cloud.
You never knew where she'd touch down,
which houses would be ripped out."

My grandmother said the Midwest
boasted more twisters than anywhere in the world.
A tornado flattened her family's barn,
lifted horses, dropped them half a mile away,
drove haystraws clear through fenceposts,
then blithely skipped over the farmhouse.

I think about chasers who make tornadoes their specialty,
study the updrafts, convection currents,
the odd clouds that prefigure a sudden spiral.
This could easily be my line of work.

I leave my brittle grandmother, her wig
and magenta lipstick applied just for my visit,
and wad the paper into a tight ball in my pocket.

When I get home I flatten it out next to the phone,
think about what I will say, *Hello, this is
your daughter. Your mother is dying
and wants you to come.*

I picture my father - a newspaper headline:
MAN LIVES IN STORM CELLAR 15 YEARS
EMERGES FIRST TIME TODAY, AN ALBINO
I dial the number, go absolutely still inside
like the wind that suddenly drops
before the twister hits.

THE SECOND FOX

She is the second fox I've found this year
at the side of the road, her body
stiffened near derelict bedsprings,
collapsed rabbit hutch, torqued tricycle,
alluvial fan of trash dumped toward the sea.

I want to chalk her outline here,
mark the loss of kin.
Her nocturnal ways completed me.
We both preferred seclusion
but she resided in gray light,
the mottled sage hills.

As I come close, fox, we overlap
in your blank eye, which stretches me
convex across the gelid lens.
I want to bury you like the first fox,
but the stench hits hard.

All I can do is drag you under sumac,
cover you with pungent serrated leaves,
your inky lips glistening in the splotched sun
like a mollusc rim in the shallows.

I touch the submerged fire of your tail,
its flame-white tip.
Already ants, devoted to you, stream in
and out your openings. Flies fill you with eggs.
Ravens will find you soon. You will not be wasted.

THE SMALL TASK

for Joyce

The fly kept you awake,
batted the ceiling
like someone's fingers
tapping the door.
He lit exhausted
on the eyelet-laced edge
of your coverlet,
began to clean himself.
You watched
his finely barbed forelegs
that gathered oil
from a hidden gland,
the way he rubbed his feet
with swift grace,
combed his antennae,
stroked his head,
his eyes that multiplied
your pale, tired face
humbled as you watched him
attend to the small task,
vigilant.
At last sleep came.
A door
you thought you'd locked
was suddenly pushed open
from the other side.

METEORA

In Meteora monks ascend
the black pillared rock
by means of a net,
like fish lifted
to harsh light,
swung out over the abyss
on a rope
hauled up by holy men.

St. Athanasios,
the founder of the monastery,
never spoke the w ord *woman,*
forbade her presence.
She belonged to
the low ground.

The saint lived in two caves.
In one he prayed
to the Mother of God.
In the other he dug his grave,
chanted through the night,
his motionless body
a landed fish
in the stone hold of visions.

Other monks saw demons
circle the cave,
grab hold of his hair,
drag him down.

I lie in the grave
before St. Athanasios,
pull him to my ribs
clasp his thighs
with my sharp pelvis,
force him
to the brittle pressure
of my kiss.
My eyes are
the dry sea of Thessaly.

The skull of the saint
rests in a silver box
in the chapel.
The monks say
when the box is opened
on sacred occasions
the skull exudes
a miraculous scent,
affirms their belief
in life after death.

I smile
from a fissure
in the rock.
The fragrance
is that of a woman.

MOUSE TOE BONE

At the Natural History Museum
a small glassed-in room
bears the sign MICROSORTING LAB.
A woman with vole-gray hair
peers alternately through
a microscope and a magnifying glass.
We gather at the window
to watch her intimate work.
She concentrates
on something we cannot see,
then chooses a sable brush
from among the sixteen
that descend in size
from her translucent pink elbow.
She whittles away with tweezers,
an array of knives and probes.
Close to the glass we see
a small nugget in the center
of a Petrie dish
with the label MOUSE TOE BONE.
Other dishes are marked
INSECT, SHELL, PLANT, BONE,
and QUESTIONS.
Her sense of order emanates
through the glass,
a territorial scent
we read with instincts
newly unearthed.
She could be sorting grain,
digging a burrow, or gnawing
through leather cord
with her sharp white incisors.
She works the lump of death
for signs of life,
gleans tiny fossils
from a tar chip
knocked off a quarter-ton cube

cut and hauled up
from La Brea tar pits.
Her obsidian eyes focus and glisten.
She could strike fire
from a flinty bone,
toss a pitch brand
into the black lake,
watch the bituminous souls
of a thousand trapped animals
ignite, flare a column
of hot light and musky smoke
at the center of the city.

She moves towards us
cups something in her palm.
We watch motionless
as she opens her hand and reveals
a tiny fluted knuckle
that she joins
to the mouse toe bone,
just turns it like a key
to fit.

LA BREA WOMAN

In the black museum case
your tar-varnished bones
recall sacred relics,
St. Polycarp's knuckles in Smyrna
or St. Anne's skull in Chartres.
Every year on the saint's day of death
known as "dies natalis,"
the relics work modest miracles:
Aunt Aurora's arthritis cured,
or cousin Paul's lost watch
turned up in the vent.

At first I have no petition,
simply stand and watch
as your bones flesh out
with soft holographic light.
Eyes fill sockets,
nose pyramids from hollow triangle,
lips fold over stark rows of teeth,
chert-black hair glimmers,
skin sheathes you,
jade beads appear,
young gourd-breasted woman,
nine thousand carbon years old.
The legend says you're the only human
discovered in tar,
among thousands of dire wolves,
mammoths, three-toed sloths,
saber-toothed tigers,
millions of dragonflies, beetles, and mice.

Then your acorn-sleek body dissolves.
Your bones speak to us.
The heart-shaped pelvis
says you are woman, man is oval.
The upper left femur gives your height,
four feet five inches.
Newly erupted wisdom teeth
say you are twenty-five.

A splintered hole at the base of your skull
reveals a death by violent blow.
You were cast into the bitumen lake,
fodder for scavengers
drawn down to the water-glazed tar.

You die and come back many times.
I want to know your name,
your words for tree, hand, jade, fire,
children, spirit, death.
I want to know the stories you told,
the reason you were struck down.
Your death and the death of your tribe
are a gray absence upon this land.

Now the tar sprawls across the basin.
Great snakes of asphalt
move us quickly to places
we no longer know.
I want you to return in me,
in the seasons,
the underground workings of water,
the seven stars that rise in winter,
the signs of rattler sheddings,
rain beetles, and great horned owls.

In the Middle Ages it was believed,
each body contained
an incorruptible seed bone,
which could reconstruct the whole.
Here is my prayer.
I carry your seed bone back to my garden,
plant you in ochre clay and wait.

AHEKI, RIVER SONG

On July 14, 1991, forty-five miles north of Lake Shasta, a Southern Pacific tanker car slipped rail at the Cantara Loop, a hairpin curve in the tracks, and dumped a broad-spectrum soil sterilizer, metam sodium, into the upper Sacramento River. The river died for forty-five miles of its length and up to a hundred feet on either side.

$$CH_3NH-C \overset{S \ominus \ Na\oplus}{\underset{S}{\Bigg\langle}} \quad + \quad H-O-H \quad \longrightarrow \quad CH_3NH-C \overset{S}{\underset{SH}{\Bigg\langle}} \quad + \quad NaOH$$

$$CH_3NH-C \overset{S}{\underset{SH}{\Bigg\langle}} \quad \longrightarrow \quad CH_3N = C = S \quad + \quad H_2S$$

Metam sodium violently takes up water as the highly active sodium atom cleaves a water molecule by bonding with the hydroxyl radical(-OH) to form sodium hydroxide, commonly known as lye or caustic soda. Left behind is the water molecule's remaining hydrogen ion (H-), which fulfills the unsatisfied sulphur bond. The resulting "metam" part of the original molecule is unstable and immediately breaks down into the primary killer substances: hydrogen sulfide, the well-known rotten-egg-smelling toxic gas; and methylisothiocyanate (MITC).

- Dr. Eric Barham

I

Aheki river, aheki dead river,
Sacramento, sacrament,
watershed of Shasta
after Sasti the chief.
In the tribe of Sasti
the word for pain
was the same as the word
for spirit, aheki.
Among the Sasti
a woman was chosen
to become a shaman
by her dream,
when the spirit stood
with bow and arrow
aimed at her heart
and commanded her to sing!
For three days and nights
the woman sang,
danced the spirit song
lodged in her heart.
She brought forth
aheki from her body,
sharp obsidian
pointed at both ends,
pressed the dark chip
into her ear, pulled it
from the other ear,
pushed it into her forehead.
The woman
who holds aheki
within
is full of spirit
when she falls down sweating,
falls down bleeding,
down moaning
river, dead river.

II

In the dream
a snake with many fangs
set one behind the other
strikes my right hand.
The snake holds on
to my writing hand
and will not let go.
I have its fangs
in my body.

III

Snake hisses poison
metam sodium, poisoned river,
snake chants the dead:
algae, horsetail, columbine,
monkeyflower, pennyroyal,
mountain violet, spreading phlox,
tiger lily, pitcher plant,
mayfly, caddisfly, mosquito,
alderfly, dragonfly,
crayfish, rainbow trout,
wild brown trout, bass,
squawfish, sculpin, suckerfish,
water ouzel, great blue heron,
osprey, red-winged blackbird,
killdeer, chickadee, hermit warbler,
bat, flying squirrel,
racoon, ringtail, otter,
mink, beaver, striped skunk,
bobcat, gray fox, coyote, black bear,
black oak, white oak, cottonwood,
madrone, maple, white fir,
juniper, red fir, sugar pine,
Pacific yew, lodgepole pine,
Douglas fir, incense cedar,
ponderosa pine, mountain hemlock.

FALSE WATER

Late at night, flocks of grebes
fall from the sky,
blown off course by stormy gusts.
Their wild eyes search
for the dark mirror of a lake
or the black-lustred ribbon of a river.
Grebes are descendants of ancient aquatic birds
unable to light on the ground,
their legs set back on bodies
streamlined for water.
Their flight is labored,
swanlike necks drooping towards earth.

The grebes mistake the wet sheen of roofs for ponds,
the slick streets for fingers of delta,
like the trick of clean glass in childhood
when the sliding backdoor I thought open
struck me and shattered,
a huge brittle bird's chest of shivered glass.
The grebes hit false water,
flop like great plumed fish,
or crumple, dying.

The whole town emerges.
We gather the living one by one
in cardboard boxes and set them beside us
on car seats or pickup truck beds
and take them down to the river they missed.
I hold a moon-breasted grebe against me,
familiar and deep as a child,
then set the bird on dark water
and watch the yellow stroke of the beak,
the white flash of the underparts,
the midnight plumage, vanish.

BEES, AFTER CHERNOBYL

My friend and I drink tea,
scoop out honey, food of the gods,
with a small silver dipper
from her mother's hive pot.
The lid's knob is cast as a bee.

She says her husband almost died
when a bee flew into his mouth
as he ate fresh shrimp on a Mexican beach.
His throat swelled shut
and the bee died on his tongue.

One hovers near my violet sweater,
puzzled when he fails
to find the center of a flower.
Sorry for the trick of color,
I would like to offer a throat of nectar,
a tongue of pollen.

Five thousand years ago,
priestesses of the bee in Ukraine,
gave thanks in hive-shaped sanctuaries,
carved her sacred form in bone.

There will be a shortage of honey this year
after Chernobyl.
Bees are especially sensitive.
The hexagonal cells in silent hives
are tombs of eggs, larvae, queens.

Rain starts up, but I hear clouds
of dead bees pelt the windows.
As a child, I feel my hand close
around the deafening gold and black creature
that drones in the vining rose.

BLUE FOR DYING, RED FOR DEATH

Trees in the Black Forest's heart
are paint-splotched blue for dying,
red for death, a terrible litmus.
The forest gives us breath.
We give off acid transfused by rain
into the dark veins of our guardians.
The alder, when felled, bleeds crimson
like a woman or a man.
We are not the stewards of this place.
We are kept by the mystery
that lives in the woods
where the sibyl tongues of branches
click and clack like wooden spatulas.
When the sacred groves were razed
in ancient Greece, the priestess cried,
"The more you eat,
the hungrier you will be!"
What is above has been severed
from what is below.
The Brothers Grimm understood
the depth of the woods
must not be trespassed.
When we paint the trees blue,
we paint our own bodies.
When we paint the trees red,
we stain our children.

TOWARD HAUSLAB PASS

The dead who come back to us in body
speak a language of dust, peat, and ice.
The Egyptian mummy reclines under glass,
a thin Nubian wind escaping his lips.
The Lindow man from Cheshire drools brown spittle,
syllables from the peaty soup of the bog.
And now the man discovered
just as we entered the dark cycle of the year.

A woman descending toward Hauslab Pass cried out
at the shrunken brown man, a bald foetus
emerging from the greenish-black slush,
his leathery skin draped on a fretwork of bones.
He mummified in the foehn, a warm dry wind,
then froze in the glacier, a chill womb
for over five thousand years.

Brought forth on the Austro-Italian border,
he grimaces, hare-lipped on the threshold of speech,
while Italian TV crews make him sit up and wave.
Disputes have arisen between the two countries
while the hikers who found him claim half his value,
with the other half for the landowner.

I want him too, secretly long to put my ear
to his lips curled back like burnt parchment
and listen to the Similaun glacier on his tongue,
trace the parallel indigo lines on his back,
decipher the small cross tattoos,
the intersection of worlds above each knee.
I covet him like a god relic
when he was simply a man who got lost and died.
And this also draws me,
the preservation of the ordinary life.

We are intimate with him,
investigate every part of his body.
Soon we will know his age, what he ate,
whether or not he gnashed his teeth in his dreams.
We will extract his genetic code
and carbon date the grass in his boots.
I want to know what spirit enlivened the stones
as he knelt near the edge of the glacier,
put down his copper ax, long bow, and quiver of fourteen arrows,
took out flint, kindling from a pouch,
and struck fire against the advancing cold.

I want to know what he murmured as he fingered
the necklace of leather strips bound with a stone,
this man who understood mountains and ice,
ore-bearing rocks, wild boar, red deer, and ma   t,
what prayers he offered exhausted,
as the strange death claimed
then released him into the baffled hands
of his distant descendants.

THE WOMAN AND THE BIRD

The woman in black
stands at the side of the road.
She stares
at the large headless bird,
its split open chest
a bloody accordion of ribs and flesh.
She turns a stone over
and over in her hand.
The woman casts no shadow.
The bird is not hawk or owl,
lacks the unsheathed talons.
The inner organs are scooped out.
Brown feather gobbets dot the hill.
She searches but cannot find the head.
Soon someone will come,
grasp the bird by its lizard-gray legs,
slide it into a plastic bag,
and plop it in a dumpster.
She does not want this death
shunted off like garbage,
wants the carcass to remain, be seen,
feed others.
The woman, a scavenger,
wants the wings
but they are held fast
by white gristle ribbons.
She kneels, strikes stone against joint,
wrenches it free.
People in cars slow down,
stare at the woman in black
who raises an enormous wing
at the side of the road.

THE SEASON OF BLUE WOLVES

THE GREEN GOD

The green god stirs in the leafy half-light
that climbs from white roots
where bones gorge on worms.
Light that first wriggles in the black soil
creeps up the capillary weave of his flesh,
each bright cell stitched whole with his body.
The green god dances the penumbra edge of things,
hands curved out toward the still sun,
a ball tossed up, arrested mid-air,
just before the moment of return.
Children balance eggs upright on walls.
Women's breasts swell with salt water.
Men hide in trees.
Underground, ants leave the giant queen alone,
cluster motionless in tunnels to listen.
Birds go silent on limbs,
fish hang suspended in a glass-surfaced sea.
When the sun moves again, the god vanishes.
Women tear their hair and weep.
Men climb down and make weapons.
Children pick up stones along the sea,
take them home and paint them green.

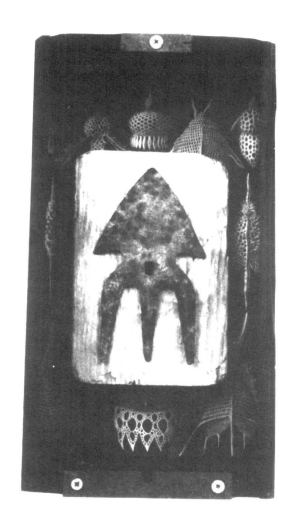

EVIDENCE

Algae multiplies
in the lightless gas tank of my car.

Sow bugs, the only dry-land crustaceans,
expire between my typewriter keys.

My husband finds linked chains of ants,
tiny suspension bridges, hung
from the fence to his car.

Cockroaches breed in my mother's clock-radio.

My daughter finds a king snake coiled
beneath the television.

Rats nest in the furnace,
which sets off small explosions
when we turn up the heat.

A raccoon tangles
with a transformer in substation 9
and knocks out the city's power.

The plumber tells me it's not a leak.
I have a spring under my house.

THE WATERY PLACE WHERE REEDS GROW

Green men poke up through the sand,
bright phalli, all new and thirsty,
reeds with ancient delta memory
of Nile springs, lapis-lazuli skiffs
that part the luminous water lilies;
viridescent corpse light come forth.

Hollow bones hiss the old longing
in jointed flesh stalks that thrive
in a sieve of fine sand holding
nothing else. What matters is light and water.
The creek, sucked up through lush wands,
is given to sun, returned to moon.

Firm finger stems augur spring,
each trembling node a place of entry,
departure. Listen, the reeds,
in their soft friction, breathe
the secret of growing,
standing green, upright, between.

SHE CONSIDERS LOVE WITH A MAN
WHO IS ALREADY PREGNANT WITH ANOTHER WOMAN

It would be like this, the pull,
that delicious bulge that stirs above your cock.
In the dream you say
you are already pregnant by another woman.
I suggest twins, even Rome
began in heat with an unlikely pair,
vestal virgin and dusky river.
Later the effluent god
bore two lusty babes to the wolf.
A future empire hung on her teats.

When your root swells with legions, with Tiber,
I push up my salty cunt,
a rank spring tide that reverses the current.
I want to give you Dioscuri,
holy rut then maculate conception.
You firm my nipple with your tongue.
Words form on the palate of the unborn
who rock with our motion.
Fingers sprout from the buds of hands,
organs bloom in a furious division of cells,
each with its own profligate memory.
We constellate deep in the night
where the blind egg revolves
in a greedy mucus of stars.

THERE

My mother warned me
never to touch myself there
nor should anyone else
touch the place she wouldn't name.
But I discovered early on
what a sweet secret food,
bad tickling thing, mute ache,
wild agitation of wings,
sleek minnow in a deep well,
fire, turbulence, white death,
grunt, howl, laughing place,
nub of bliss, slippery berm,
mudpie, pink mollusc,
purple sea hare, Sargasso drift,
lips of drowsy moose straining rushes,
waterspout, rosy prow of Isis,
civet cat, cognoscente cunning
thing it is.

THE LOCUST, THE BEE, AND THE SPIDER

Sometimes at night
my skull softens
like damp clay in Tunisia
lying in wait for the single locust
who will make the swarm
sinking her long pointed abdomen
into my brain
depositing eggs
cuneiform in the gray flesh.
My skull softens
like warm wax in the hive
where the bee squirms
among dark hexagonal cells
thick with honey and stiff white larvae.
The spider knits
in the flesh of my palm
nesting her young between my fingers
making a womb of my hand.
I lie very still in my bed
generous as a corpse.
When the sun rises
we will all begin to hatch.

SWOLLEN MOON / NIGHT BIRTH

Though you prepare a basket with soft blankets
for the mother cat who waddles through your house,
her white belly a swollen moon between thin ebony legs,
she ignores the basket for the deepest corner
under your bed where the lost things gather.
Awakened by guttural cries late at night, you kneel,
find the missing gray sock, the child's small red ball,
The House of Spirits, a gold filigreed earring,
and a moist stillborn kitten. The mother
in rhythmic contractions releases another three
soggy creatures more rodent than cat,
their trembling whiskered heads, sealed eyes, translucent ears. You're
faintly repulsed by the glistening birth-spew,
the mother who eats each sac, licks every puling kitten,
even the one that died widening the passage for others.
You cup your hands around the dead kitten
and bury it in the mulchy soil under the pear.
Later when you kneel and peer at the cat,
your grief loosens, tears salty as amniotic waters
breaking from the place she has opened in you.

A SILK CHEMISE

When I put on a silk chemise in Venice,
I enter my longing, also yours,
to leave and return rich with the other
or to wait as trees know how to wait.
I climb pungent mulberry branches
veiled with cocoons of patient worms
that spin and wind around Polo's house,
drape his windows, compass his maps.
You leave with ships, charts, and sextant,
measure our distances by desire, the angles
between bodies of light and horizon.
You want to find your bearings in me
even as you set course for the east.
I watch for you from the tops of trees
where all movement has stilled,
except for the random twitch of pupae.
By day I pull out strands to the spindle,
prolonged lust for your salty skin,
a design I work to the shuttle rhythm
of ships weaving in and out of swells,
turned toward home after years of absence.
I imagine a cargo, bright bolts of cloth,
stories you tell me that find their ways
into my hems, seams, and exquisite lace borders.
By night I faithfully undo this hope,
watch my despair become habit.
You will not return the same man
I reconstruct day after day, unravel night after night.
When you finally appear, only the scar is familiar.
You open the hold and moths are loosed
in stuttering circles of flight.
You say you have longed for our bed
built around an ancient oak,
hung with a white canopy
like a mast fitted out with sails.
I let fall the silk chemise
which lies on the floor, crumpled
like the damp new wings of a moth,
then slowly unfurls.
Already I dream of my own departure
while you wait with a strange silence.
Your feet have begun to take root.

SEVEN BEAUTIFUL WOMEN

Flying fish rise from the black sea
that curves into sky,
toward the light
cast by our starboard window,
drift and fan long fin-wings,
sleeves of pleated silk.

Once, you saw their razor-thin wings
draw sequins of blood
from a fisherman's arms as he knelt
to his work on the purse seine.

You loosen my silver kimono
as I loosen yours, our icthyic motions,
a sleek skittish dance
toward the petite morte.

Overhead seven beautiful women,
the Pleiades, swim in the night.
Once the dead had to speak their names
in order to pass to the other side.

Now we living utter our cries
between worlds
as fish fly past our window.

ARTICHOKES

We prepared our dinner
of curried omelettes, artichokes,
and a dark green bottle
of Ceylonese Arak.
I unfolded
brown paper packets of spices,
saffron, cumin, turmeric, cardamom,
smells palpable
as your hair and skin.
Our movements were round
as eggs in the bowl,
prickly as
the thistle's hidden center.
We pulled away
thorned leaf by leaf,
savored each part.
Under the gauze
of mosquito netting
on the broad bed,
I undid the crisp silk pleats
of my sari.
You fell open, bristling.
Our fingers, sore and red,
found the heart.

LUPINES

bleed the hillsides blue
like wolves that burst
the jugular veins of spent animals.
Lapis lazuli spills from their throats.
The eyes
are white jets of flame.
Blue wolves stalk
the sun and the moon.
They range from the vase
on my kitchen table,
circle the winter fire
that sputters under my breath.
I fight to keep spring at bay
but the small fire dies.
The ferocity that blooms
on the hills
moves into my body
stains my skin
like the indigo cloth
of the Blue Women
in the Sahara.
The only color
that stirs in the desert.
Lupine blue, my only color,
turns toward the light.

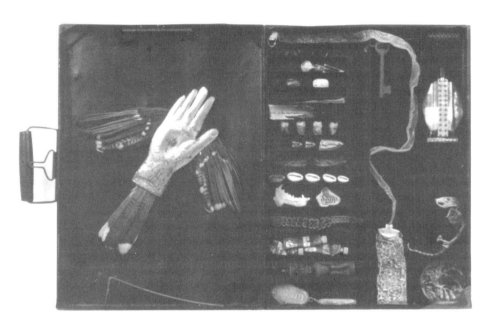

VANESSA CARDUI*

All day the painted ladies skitter through my yard,
scraps of orange paper, the handbills of spring.
They flock down the spicy eucalyptus hill,
dip to the pool, then up through yellow-tasseled acacia,
Canary Island pines, and flicker toward gray mountains
that lift above the smudge line of smog.

I watch them from my window,
as I wake fever-dry between fitful naps.
The quirky kite tail of ladies skips north,
driven by a procreant butterfly binge
on mallow flower, tree sap, carrion, and scat.

Vanessa cardui signals a lush end
to the drought I have also felt within,
aridity Hildegard of Bingen called the greatest sin.
The abbess encouraged her ladies of the convent
to don brocades, enfold themselves in silks,
wear gold and jewels to reflect back creation.

As the fever breaks, I rise from my bed,
stand naked and damp before the mirror
while the ladies approach, their wings
mapped with orange fields, dark mountains,
underwings pearled with the glow of eyespots.
They swirl and settle on my wan skin,
drape me with the wild praise of their wings.

*Species name for the painted lady, a butterfly whose numbers
fluctuate greatly from years of scarcity to a single year of enormous
abundance.

ABOUT THE AUTHOR

Regina O'Melveny is a writer, assemblage artist, and teacher. Her poetry and prose have been anthologized and widely published in literary magazines such as *The Jacaranda Review, Yellow Silk, Poetry/LA, The Sun, The LA Weekly, The Pittsburgh Quarterly*, and *The Wild Duck Review*. In 1995 she won first place in the John Foster West National Poetry Award Contest, judged by Marge Piercy. Recently she was a finalist in the *Salt Hill Journal* Poetry Contest and she was given an International Merit Award from the *Atlanta Review*. Her work has been performed on radio KUSC FM Los Angeles, as well as choreographed and performed by the San Pedro City Ballet at the Western Regional Dance Conference in Washington. A selection of her poems and artwork was shown at the exhibit "Assemblage '95, Personal Icons," at the Harbor College Art Gallery in San Pedro. She has been awarded writer's residency fellowships by the Dorland Mountain Arts Colony in California and the Cummington Community of the Arts in Massachusetts. She lives with her husband, daughter, and many animals in the coastal sage-scrub hills of Rancho Palos Verdes, California.

Blue Wolves was designed and composed by Bertha Rogers, using Adobe Pagemaker 6.0. The typeface is Goudy Old Style. The book was printed on 60-lb. offset, acid-free, recycled paper in the United States of America by the Courier Printing Corporation, Deposit, New York. This first edition is limited to copies in paper wrappers.

OTHER BRIGHT HILL PRESS BOOKS

Speaking the Words Anthology
Edited by Bertha Rogers

The Word Thursdays Anthology
Edited by Bertha Rogers

The Man Who Went Out for Cigarettes
Adrian Blevins-Church
Winner, 1995 Bright Hill Press
Poetry Chapbook Competition

Iroquois Voices, Iroquois Visions:
A Celebration of Contemporary Six Nations Arts
Edited by Bertha Rogers.
Contributing Editors: Maurice Kenny, Tom Huff,
Robert Bensen

My Own Hundred Doors
Pam Bernard
Winner, 1995-96 Bright Hill Press
Poetry Book Award

Low Country Stories
Lisa Harris
Winner, 1996 Bright Hill Press
Fiction Chapbook Competition

Out of the Catskills and Just Beyond:
Literary and Visual Works by Catskill Writers and Artists,
with a Special Section by Catskill High-School Writers and Artists
Edited by Bertha Rogers